To: Michael 7/19/2021

Happy [illegible]

I Love you very much!

Love, Mom

To

____

Best wishes from

____

____

Your birth was one of the amazing events of 1981.

Within these pages are some other interesting, earth-shattering moments of the year that was 1981.

Enjoy!

1981 Celebrated the
Marriage of Prince
Charles to Lady
Diana Spencer

IT HAPPENED IN JANUARY, 1981

BORN IN 1981

• The largest known underground caving system - Sarawak Chamber was discovered in The Borneo.

• Greece enters the European Economic Community.

• Hitchhiker's Guide to the Galaxy' first airs on BBC2 in the UK.

• Pope John Paul II has a meeting with Lech Walesa, the Polish Solidarity leader at the Vatican

• In the UK, Peter Sutcliffe otherwise known as 'The Yorkshire Ripper' is arrested in Sheffield. He was later convicted of murdering 13 women.

• Irish civil rights leader Bernadette Devlin McAliskey was shot by loyalists.

• Rupert Murdoch, the Australian media tycoon agrees to buy 'The Times'.

• Iranian officials release 52 American hostages after 14 months in captivity.

• The first DeLorean car, later made famous by the 'Back to the Future' movies comes off the production line in Northern Ireland.

BORN IN 1981

• An earthquake in China kills 150.

• Madame Mao, fourth wife of The Chairman of the Communist Party in The People's Republic of China is sentenced to death.

• Massive floods in South Africa wipe away the town of Lainsburg.

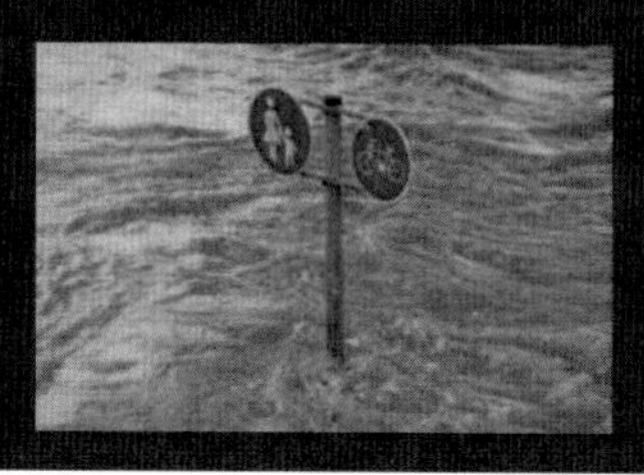

• In the Java Sea, an Indonesian passenger ship capsizes killing 580 people.

IT HAPPENED IN FEBRUARY, 1981

BORN IN 1981

• 21 football fans are killed and 54 injured after a stampede at an Olympiacos & AEK Athens game.

• In the UK, Prime Minister Margaret Thatcher announces the part privatisation of British Aerospace.

• In Dublin, a devastating fire at a nightclub kills 48 people and injures another 200.

• The British National Coal Board announces widespread pit closures.

• Australia withdraws recognition of the Pol Pot regime in Cambodia.

• Tensions rise in Northern Ireland.

• Charles, Prince of Wales announces his engagement to 19 year old Lady Diana Spencer.

• Pope John Paul II pays a visit to the Philippines.

• In America, the National Hockey League saw the highest number of penalties in a game between Bruins v Northstars with 84 penalties in the game.

• American President, Ronald Reagan meets with British Prime Minister, Margaret Thatcher in Washington DC.

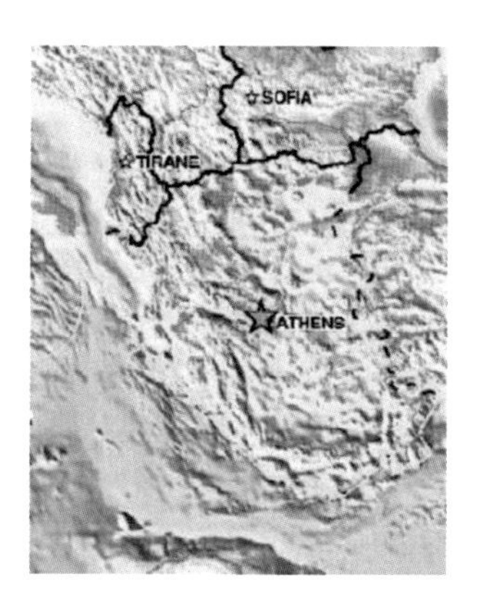

• A powerful earthquake hits Athens.

• Rupert Murdoch buys The Times and The Sunday Times

• The Archbishop of Canterbury advises the Church of England to view homosexuality as a 'handicap' and not a sin.

IT HAPPENED IN MARCH, 1981

• Walter Cronkite retires from CBS Evening News after 19 years of hosting the programme

• The ZX81, the first ever mass market home computer is launched by Sinclair Research selling over one and a half million units.

• In Northern Ireland, IRA member Bobby Sands goes on hunger strike.

• The iconic Tom Baker who played Doctor Who leaves the series after seven and a half years.

BORN IN 1981

- Unemployment in the UK hits 2.4 million.
- In the USA, three workers are killed whilst working on the Space Shuttle Columbia.

- Rumblings start about ousting Margaret Thatcher as Prime Minister.
- In Chile, Augusto Pinochet is sworn in as President.
- American President Ronald Reagan is shot in the chest and badly injured by John Hinckley jr.
- The first London Marathon starts with just 7500 runners.

- Robert Redford's movie 'Ordinary People' wins 'Best Picture' & 'Best Director' during the 53rd Academy Awards

IT HAPPENED IN APRIL, 1981

• In Dublin, the Eurovision Song Contest is won by British pop band 'Buck's Fizz' with their song 'Making your Mind Up'.

• In the UK, Rioters attack police officers and loot shops causing massive damage in Brixton, South London.

• In California, the Space Shuttle Columbia launches With NASA astronauts John Young and Robert Crippen in the first manned reusable spacecraft.

- IRA member on hunger strike in the Maze prison, Northern Ireland, is elected MP for Fermanagh and South Tyrone in a by election.
- Unemployment in the UK passes 2,500,000 for the first time in 50 years.

- Steve Davis wins the 1981 World Snooker Championship.

- Peter Sutcliffe admits to the manslaughter of 13 women on the grounds of diminished responsibility.

IT HAPPENED IN MAY, 1981

• In Vienna, law students from West Germany, Austria, Poland and Hungary create The European Law Student's Association.

• In Northern Ireland Republican Bobby Sands dies aged 27 in prison after having been on hunger strike for 66 days. Three more die over the coming weeks.

• Jamaican singer, Bob Marley dies age 36 from cancer.

• The 100th FA Cup final ends with a draw between Manchester United and Tottenham Hotspur at Wembley Stadium.

• Pope John Paul II is shot and nearly killed as he addresses an audience at St Peter's Square in The Vatican City. The pope later recovers.

• In London, Andrew Lloyd Webber's first performance of his musical Cats is shown at The New London Theatre.

• Socialist Francois Mitterand becomes the first socialist President of the French Fifth Republic.

• In the UK, Peter Sutcliffe is found guilty of being the Yorkshire Ripper after having murdered 13 women.

• Alain Robert scales the Willis Tower in Chicago.

• The whole Italian government resigns over a link to a fascist party

• The Gulf Cooperation Council is created between Saudi Arabia, Oman, Qatar, Bahrain and the United Arab Emirates.

• The Bangladeshi president is assassinated.

• In London, up to 100,000 people march to Trafalgar Square for the 'TUC's March for Jobs'

• Liverpool FC wins the European Cup by beating Real Madrid in France.

IT HAPPENED IN JUNE, 1981

• The first recognized cases of medical conditions that weaken immune systems in homosexual men were recorded in Los Angeles, leading eventually to the first recognized cases of AIDS.

• In the UK, Shergar wins the Epsom Derby

• A train crash in India kills hundreds.

• In the UK, political parties 'The Liberal Party' and the 'SDP' form an alliance.

• An Israeli air strike in Iraq kills ten Iraqi troops raising tension levels in the area.

• Aircraft carrier HMS Ark Royal is launched in Newcastle, England.

• 'Raiders of the Lost Ark' starring Harrison Ford is released.

• A Brit fired six blank gunshots at Queen Elizabeth II as she rode down The Mall to the Trooping of The Colour Ceremony.

• The 'Organisation of Eastern Caribbean States' is founded.

• In the UK, unemployment reaches nearly 2,700,000 – one in nine of the workforce.

• In Nevada, the Lockheed F-117 Stealth Fighter takes its maiden flight.

• Paintball is played for the first time in the United States.

• John McEnroe launches his 'You cannot be serious!' tirade at the umpire in his first round match at Wimbledon.

IT HAPPENED IN JULY, 1981

• Riots in Toxteth, Liverpool start after tensions rise between police and local youths. Further riots occur in Leeds and other cities across the UK. Prime Minister Margaret Thatcher approves the use of rubber bullets, water cannon and armoured vehicles to quell the civil unrest. The riots are blamed on the government's economic policies which have seen unemployment rise dramatically in the UK.

• In the United States, President Ronald Reagan appoints Sandra Day O'Connor to the Supreme Court of The United States. She was the first woman to hold the position.

• Nintendo release 'Donkey Kong', which along with 'Super Mario' would become some of the most successful computer games ever produced.

• 114 people are killed in Kansas City when a Hyatt Regency skywalk collapses.

• In the UK, British Leyland ceases production of the Austin Maxi motor car.

• Israel bomb Beirut killing many civilians resulting in worldwide condemnation of their actions.

• In Mexico City, the first panda was born in captivity – the first to be born outside of China.

• The wedding of Prince Charles to Lady Diana Spencer occurred at St Paul's Cathedral in London. A record TV audience watched the wedding.

• A massive demonstration occurred in Lodz in Communist Poland protesting over food shortages in the country.

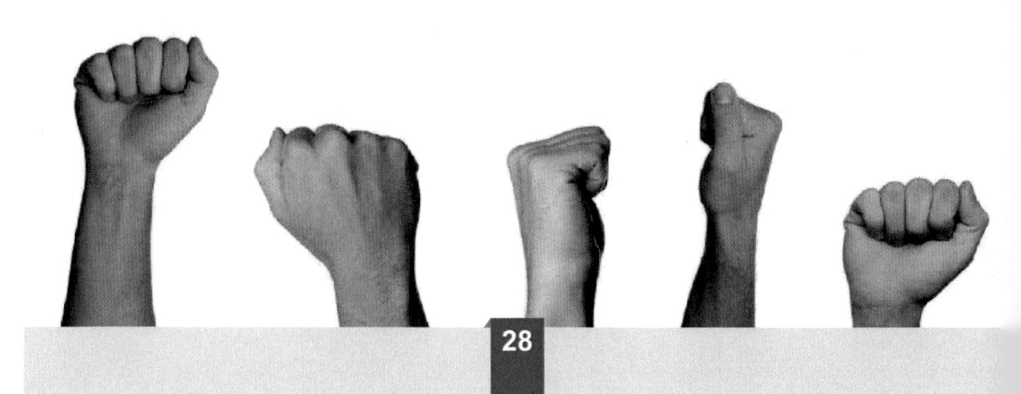

IT HAPPENED IN AUGUST, 1981

• The first 24 hour video music channel is launched - MTV (Music Television). The first video aired was 'Video Killed The Radio Star' by 'The Buggles'.

• Further IRA hunger strikers die in prison.

• In the United States, the original Model 5150 IBM Personal Computer was launched at a cost of $1565.

• US fighter jets destroy two Libyan fighter jets over the Gulf of Sidra.
• The Vauxhall Cavalier is launched by General Motors in the UK.

• Mark David Chapman is imprisoned for the murder of John Lennon.

• In Iran, the Iranian President & senior ministers are killed in a terrorist bomb attack.

• Another bomb attack in Ramstein, West Germany injures 20 people at a US Air Force base.

• In the UK, Moira Stuart aged 29 becomes the BBC's first black news reader.

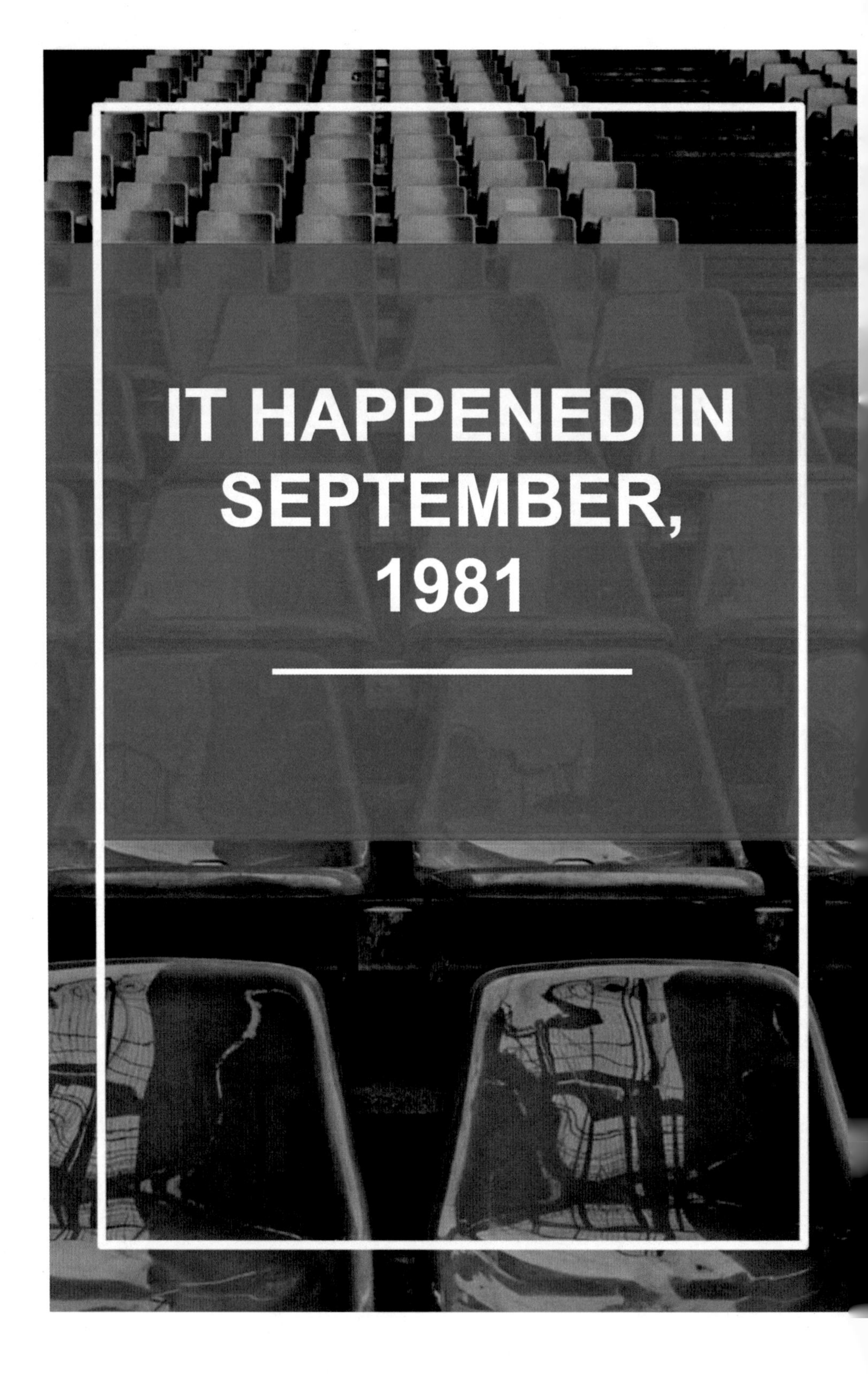

IT HAPPENED IN SEPTEMBER, 1981

• An explosion at a mine in Czechoslovakia kills 65 people.
• The highly popular British sitcom 'Only Fools & Horses & Horses' first airs in the UK.

• France abolishes capital punishment.
• Nearly half a million people attend a free 'Simon & Garfunkel' concert in Central Park, New York

• The Boeing 767 airliner makes its maiden flight

• The Rolling Stones begin their 'Tattoo You' tour at the JFK Stadium in Philadelphia.

• In France, a high speed rail service between Lyon & Paris begins.

• Children's series 'Danger Mouse' & 'Postman Pat' debuts on UK TV.

• In Australia, the Sydney Tower opens to the public for the first time.

• Off the coast of Norway a team of divers start recovering £40 million of gold ingots from the sunk wreck of 'HMS Edinburgh'

- A Solidarity Day March in support of organized Labour draws around 250,000 people in Washington DC.

- Belize is granted Independence

- Liverpool Football Club mourns the loss of manager, Bill Shankly who dies aged 67 years old.

IT HAPPENED IN OCTOBER, 1981

- Iconic English pop band 'The Police' release their album 'Ghost in the Machine'.
- In Northern Ireland, the Maze Prison hunger strike comes to an end
- The Provisional IRA bomb Chelsea Barracks

- Egyptian President, Anwar Sadat is assassinated. One week later, Hosni Mubarak is elected as President of Egypt.

- Gas explosions at a coal mine in Japan leave 93 people dead.
- The new Prime Minister of Greece is Andreas Papandreou
- CND Anti Nuclear March in London attracts 250,000 protesters

- A soviet submarine runs aground near to a Swedish military base.

IT HAPPENED IN NOVEMBER, 1981

• Antigua and Barbuda gain independence from the United Kingdom

• In the UK, car manufacturer British Leyland's 58,000 work force go out on strike over pay and conditions.

• The Church of England General Synod agrees to admit women into holy orders

• The England football team beat Hungary 1-0 at Wembley Stadium to qualify for the 1982 World Cup. The first time they have qualified since 1970.

England  **Von links: Keegan, Clemence, McDermott, Mariner, Osman, Francis, Thompson, Neal, Mills, Hoddle, Robson.**

• United States President Ronald Reagan authorizes the CIA to recruit and support Contra rebels in Nicaragua.

• Buckingham Palace announces the Princess of Wales's pregnancy.

• Britain is hit by 105 tornadoes in a single night

IT HAPPENED IN DECEMBER, 1981

• An aircraft crashes into a mountain in Corsica killing all 180 people on board.

• In the UK, Arthur Scargill becomes President Elect of the National Union of Mineworkers

• The first case of AIDS is diagnosed in the UK.

• In boxing, in his last ever fight Muhammad Ali loses to Trevor Berbick

• In El Salvador the army kill 900 civilians in the El Mozote massacre

• In Beirut, a car bomb destroys the Iraqi Embassy killing 61 people.

• In the UK, the Penlee Life Boat disaster occurs off the Cornish coast.

• The first ever test tube baby, Elizabeth Jordan Carr was born in Norfolk.

• Severe snow storms hit the UK as temperatures drop to their lowest levels since the 1870's.

AMERICAN BILLBOARD BEST-SELLING SINGLES OF 1981

- 'Bette Davis Eyes' by Kim Carnes
- 'Endless Love' by Diana Ross & Lionel Richie
- 'Lady' by Kenny Rogers
- '(Just Like) Starting Over' by John Lennon
- 'Jessie's Girl' by Rick Springfield
- 'Celebration' by Kool & The Gang
- 'Kiss on my List' by Hall & Oates
- '9 to 5' by Dolly Parton
- 'Keep on Loving You' by REO Speedwagon

BRITISH BEST-SELLING SINGLES OF 1981

- 'Tainted Love' by Soft Cell
- 'Stand & Deliver' by Adam and the Ants
- 'Prince Charming' by Adam and the Ants
- 'This Ole House' by Shakin' Stevens
- 'Vienna' by Ultravox
- 'One Day In Your life' by Michael Jackson
- 'Making Your Mind Up' by Bucks Fizz
- 'Shaddap Your Face' by Joe Dolce
- 'You Drive Me Crazy' by Shakin' Stevens

BRITISH BEST-SELLING ALBUMS OF THE YEAR 1981

- Kings of The Wild Frontier' - Adam And The Ants
- 'Greatest Hits' - Queen
- 'Dare' – The Human League
- 'Face Value' – Phil Collins
- 'Shaky' – Shakin' Stevens
- 'Ghost In The Machine' – The Police
- 'Love Songs' – Cliff Richard
- 'Chart Hits 1981' – Various Artists
- 'Prince Charming' – Adam And The Ants
- 'Double Fantasy' – John Lennon & Yoko Ono

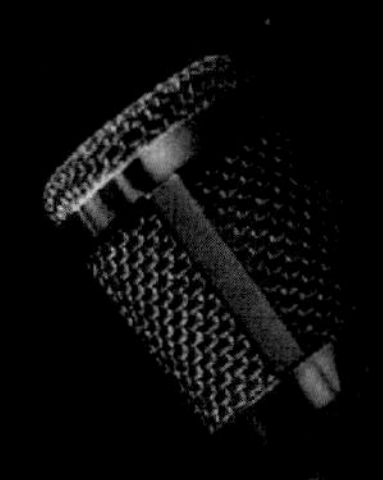

BRITISH HIGHEST GROSSING FILMS OF 1981

1. Raiders Of The Lost Ark
2. Excalibur
3. Popeye
4. An American Werewolf in London
5. Clash Of The Titans
6. Ordinary People
7. Friday the 13th Part 2
8. Superman II
9. For Your Eyes Only
10. Stir Crazy

NORTH AMERICAN HIGHEST GROSSING FILMS OF 1981

1. Raiders Of The Lost Ark
2. On Golden Pond
3. Superman II
4. Arthur
5. Stripes
6. The Cannonball Run
7. Chariots of Fire
8. For Your Eyes Only
9. The Four Seasons
10. Time Bandits

SPORTING ACHIEVEMENTS OF 1981

• Hana Mandlíková won the French Open Tennis title - one of the four grand slam wins of her career.

• Tracy Austin won her second US Open Tennis title defeating Martina Navratilova.

• John McEnroe won Wimbledon and the US Open and eventually retired from competitive tennis the following year.

• Tom Watson won the Masters Tournament for his fifth major and Larry Nelson won his first major taking the PGA Championship. Sandra Haynie won the du Maurier Classic for the fourth and final major title of her career.

• Nelson Piquet won the Formula 1 driver's championship by a single point, one of the smallest margin wins ever.

• The Super Bowl was won by Oakland in New Orleans

• Tottenham Hotspur beat Manchester City in the FA Cup

• The Tennis French Open was won by Hana Mandlikova and Bjorn Borg.

• David Graham won the Gold US Open

• In July, the Tour de France was won by Bernard Hinault

• The Golf British Open was won by Bill Rogers

• The Baseball World Series was won by the Los Angeles Dodgers

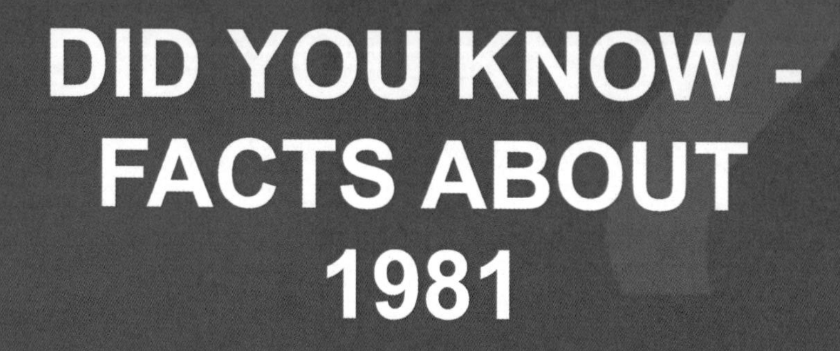
DID YOU KNOW -
FACTS ABOUT
1981

Cost of living in the UK in 1981

- Average house price was £30,778
- The average salary was £ 5,129
- The price of the average family car was £4,050
- A litre of fuel cost £0.35
- A weekly grocery shop cost £4.98
- Bread cost £0.41
- Sugar was £0.39 a kilo
- Milk was £0.70 a pint
- Butter was £0.47 for a 250g pack
- Cheese was £0.91 for a 400g pack

The Cost of living in North America in 1981

- 2% milk was $1.64 a gallon
- A 3lb bag of apples was $1.19
- Sliced white bread was 59 cents a loaf
- Broccoli cost 39 cents per pound
- Flour was 89 cents for 5 pound bag
- White sliced bread 59 cents
- Ground Beef cost $1.86 per pound
- Potatoes were $1.25 for a 10 pound bag
- The Atari Home Video game station cost up to $179. The games cost $19.99 each
- A movie theatre ticket cost $2.00.
- A new house cost just under $84,600.
- A new Datsun Stanza cost $6,680.
- Renting a movie at Blockbuster cost about $8. Membership fee was $50
- A video cassette recorder would cost between $599 & $950

1981: THE BEST AND THE WORST

- The ZX81, a pioneering British home computer is launched by 'Sinclair Research' going on to sell one and a half million units worldwide.

- Nintendo launches 'Donkey Kong' featuring the debut of 'Mario'.

- The IBM Personal computer is launched

- Five hundred are killed in India when a train plunges into the Baghmati River

- Dr Michael Harrison of the University of California performs the worlds first open fetal surgery.

- The AIDS pandemic begins in the United States

- The first heart-lung transplant is undertaken at Stanford Hospital

- Two walkways collapsed at The Hyatt Regency in Kansas City killing 114 and injuring another 216 people. At the time, it was the deadliest structural collapse in US history.

- Space Shuttle: Columbia had its first launch

POPULAR IN 1981...............

- Big phones

- Big hair

- The TV show 'Brideshead Revisited'
- 'Greed is Good' attitude
- Pastel suits
- Cabbage Patch Kids
- Smurfs
- Rubik's cubes
- My Little Pony
- Leggings
- Yuppies
- Cassette Tapes

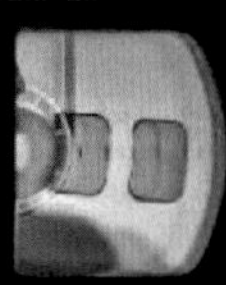

- Shoulder pads
- Pac Man
- Princess Diana

REMEMBERING BOB MARLEY............

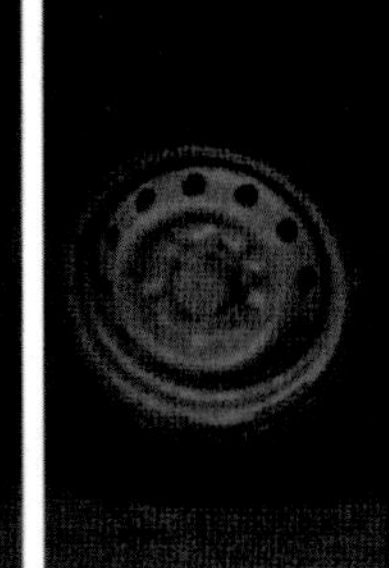

- 1981 will sadly be remembered by many as the year that Bob Marley died.

- Starting with his band 'The Wailer's' in 1964 he later pursued a highly successful solo career in 1974.

- In 1977 he released 'Exodus' which went on to sell 75 million copies worldwide and included such hits as 'Jamming' and 'One Love'.

- In 1978, he then released the best-selling album 'Kaya' which included the singles 'Is this Love' and 'Satisfy My Soul'.

- A committed Rastafarian he infused his music with a mix of good feeling and happy spirituality. He is credited with popularizing reggae music and serves as an ongoing symbol of Jamaican culture and identity.

- After his death in 1984, his greatest hits album 'Legend' became the biggest selling reggae album of all time.

Made in the USA
Columbia, SC
25 June 2021